LoveLife6958

Memoirs from the pen...

GW01066381

By Chris Syrus

ISBN 978-1-907188-08-4
Copyright Notice
© 2009 Christopher Syrus
All Rights Reserved

This book is dedicated to my son Kyrese Syrus
&
My mother Elaine Syrus

Forward

My first set back came with my poor exam grades.
I didn't put in the work and as a result I left school with only 2 GCSEs.

Throughout my teenage years I had a varied work history,
I became frustrated with minimum wage. I witnessed what I felt to be prejudice
in the work place and believed that there was no gain in working for others,
especially when promotion was unlikely.

I was always involved with music.
Alongside Rohan and Amanda we formed the group 'Urban Twist',
which was a mix of Hip Hop, Reggae and Soul.
We had management behind us and we were performing nationwide.

This was the hard working, dedicated, positive me at my best.
The other side was doubtful, impatient and becoming
more intrigued with easy riches. I felt in order to be successful,
I either had to make it in music or be a criminal.

On a Wednesday morning of October 2003,
Trident (police unit set up for black on black crime)
ordered me to get out of bed and get dressed.
This was the first time I had received such a request.
Unfortunately, it would not be the last.

On the 21st of January 2004, at Kingston Crown Court,
10 out of the 11 jury members,
found me guilty of 'Conspiracy to Import Class A.'
A woman was also found guilty, 2 male co-defendants had already
pleaded guilty and 1 male defendant was found not guilty.

The system re-christened me LL6958. In my fight to reclaim my identity, I have
turned this statistical brand into LoveLife6958.

Introduction

These poems are a collection of words and thoughts that I had throughout my prison sentence.

Brother page 15, refers to my blood brother who is serving his 3rd sentence for robbery. We are both fathers now, with an example to set and no more time to waste.

In Ere page 16, was originally a rap. I can remember up to 10 men, in and outside of the cell, singing along to the chorus, with a passion, at the reality of the words.

Rastaman's Cell page 18, is about moving into a Rastaman's cell and realising that a Muslim lived in the cell to the left and an Atheist in the cell to the right. My faith in a merciful and gracious God has always given me strength throughout my life.

Cry For The Dead page 27, is for a close and personal friend of mine who, like me, saw no fruits in a legitimate way of life. He swallowed drugs, which unfortunately burst in his stomach. He died travelling on the aeroplane back to England. His daughter is a great dancer (takes after him) and very beautiful, she celebrated her 7th birthday recently (2009).

The Letter page 31, refers to my twin sister. My decisions meant I was not around when she was pregnant or when she had my beautiful, intelligent niece Reneya.

If even one of these poems touch a young person's consciousness and makes them reconsider easy riches, makes them value their life and their blessed existence.
Then it is worth it.

These are my 'Memoirs from the pen...'

Contents

Mother's Cry

And I never heard
My mother cry out in pain,
Until I heard the juror
Say "Guilty."

I imagine it to be different
From the joyful yell of child birth,
Bearing twins.

The cry haunts me.
Day and night it haunts me.

Every time I'm offered a deal
Or have an idea
Of making that quick money...

It haunts me.

If only I could take back time,
The gift not given.

If only I could
Reverse the state of play
And do something different,

Choose better, wiser!

But now is not the time
To reflect in regret and hindsight,

Now is the time to make better.

Time to grow and remember,
What has happened in the past.

God willing (Insha'Allah)
I will never hear that cry again.

Locked Up

Syrus locked up.
Trying to figure out,
What I've done so hot!

Picture a normal day,
Dealing with normal drama.

Some extra ordinary shit,
Come messed up my karma.

I'm off to the station,
To answer some questions.

I only know "No comment,"
So don't ask me no questions.

Like, "What do you think?"
And "What do you reckon?"

Syrus don't inform
And Syrus don't play second.

Never been innocent,
I'm born black guilty.

Had an alibi,
But the jury found me.

Judge gave 10 and 9 to my codees,
1 bus case, scar face, he's a Yardie.

Listen… I'm in jail my friend.

My life's a bunk bed
And this Gilbert Pen.

I got a,
Big case and a lot of pride,

I've got 2 codees
And a brother inside,

I'm on the,
B wing on the 4th floor.

I've got a deja vu,
Like I've been here before.

Now I'm off to the gym.

Syrus on the road…
Na, Syrus missing.

Bus case on appeal
And you'll see him again,

Having up road
And riding rhythm.

Let's Bus Case

"I will" I said,
"Appeal" I said.

"Surely the judge
Is off his wig" I said.

Borrowed flows I did.

Just for the introduction,
Welcome to the function,
Gun butts and truncheon.

If it's not them,
It's the jealous competition,

Wishing on your downfall,
That's their only mission.

Signs of the beast!
Sirens blazing,

Juries amazing,

If only they knew
What I was facing.

If only they knew
That time's not waiting.

Waiting for the children,
Waiting for the old.

Waiting for the community
As a whole.

Na, time's a moving,

It's not only me,
It's them that's losing.

I wanted to contribute,
Bun out on confusion,

Wanted to illuminate
On all of the illusion.

Trident running through
The building,

Black on black crime,
What's the reason?

Still not even,
Damiola Taylor, Steven,
Why the Shakespeare twin
Stop breathing?

Now I'm in handcuffs leaving.

Not a statistic,
I'm a human being,

Now you know
How I'm Feeling.

Let's bus case!

The Visit

Heart broken really,
Found you nearly,
But I'm a keep looking,
If you're not for me.

Fashion sense,
I could sense
That we wasn't in season.

But I couldn't figure why
And I needed a reason.

I felt like I saw you,
In all of my dreams,

But in reflection
You were there,

Just part of the scene.

I didn't put you there,
You entered at free will.

I can't keep you there,
You're gonna be there until.

The wind or the mood,
Takes you away.

But the hour we shared,
Really made my day.

Prison Window

A purple, blue and grey sky,
Bordering the silhouette
Of the buildings outside.

Smoggy, jagged edges
Like a graph giving facts.
Homes, businesses, industrial artefacts.

It's the same sky overseas,
Framing seas in the West Indies.

It's the sky of sun and water,
Cool and warm decisive air.

My horizon, my horizon…
Oh my future and my past.

The clouds make shapes,
As planes hum
And birds sing in communication.

Is there a vision for me to see?
Horses, dragons, a way home.

There's no moon,
I call it dusk,
It's a beautiful night.

The wind called me and I looked,
To take in this glorious sight.

Love Life

I love life,
I had a real crush.

I've lived 25 years,
But that's not enough.

I give thanks
When the sun,
Comes up
Every morning,

Even when the rain
Comes pouring.

Had my hurdles
And more than
My fair share.

Give thanks to the Lord,
I'm just happy to be here.

Like I'm a celebrity,
Get me the F out of here.

So I can get back,

To the Motherland
And grow my hair.

Lullaby

I'm a rhyming fool,
But my pen is my clarity.

If I don't fear death,
How can this world get the best of me?

"Why write about it then,
Tell me why would you bother?"

Well it's my daily exercise,
Like treadmill to a jogger.

"Amaze me then,
Let me see what you've got."

I snatch this stirring off my mind
And rock it gently in this cot,

Singing, hush little baby,
Don't you cry.

That anger, that rebellion,
That won't get you by.

Humming rest picture painter,
Let the tool do its work.

We were born crying and hungry
So we're used to the hurt.

Tragedy

From the greatest tragedy,
Comes the greatest triumph.

I know some akhoy(a)s,
That are down to riot.

I know the system,
Wanna keep me quiet.

But I'm agro,
Like come on try it.

I'm agro,
Like come on try it!

The Yard

Stepping out into this,
Circular outdoor cage.

Is like jumping into the
Deep end of a shark pool.

Pre-formed groups,
Gather around the metal gate.

Athletes jog around the yard,
Their minds somewhere else.

Peacocks circle, their chest high,
Intimidating the competition.

Others walking, talking, planning.

On some mornings,
This will be the first time out of
Cell in 24 hours,

Because Social & Domestic
Was cancelled again,
Due to staff shortages.

Alliances are made on this yard.

A disrespect amongst your circle,
Is a direct disrespect to you.

Your retaliation or lack of it,
Will send messages,
Seven fold throughout the system.

If I moved to you.
It was not because I didn't value
Your life or reputation,

It was because I valued my own more.

The prisoners out number
The guards here.

They sit two up in a small cage,
Within this larger cage.

We circle and look at them,
They sit still and look at us.

If a parcel comes over the wall,
They will be powerless.

They can only take the details,
Of the donkey sent to collect it.

They could call for back up,
And end the morning exercise early.

Here there is great
Strength in numbers.

Area codes, religion and colour,
Can be the quickest identifying factor
In which to find your group.

You'll need a group,
You'll need a friend.

With time,
Cell mates bond,
Strangers bond,

People with great differences,
That would never have bonded
Previously, bond.

This is a shared experience.
Our enemy,
The system.

As A Man

As a man,
I'll never get used to
Being asked to strip.

Asked to lower my boxers,
To my knees and shake them.

As a man,
I'll never get used to
Being woken up abruptly,

Led down to the testing suite,
And ordered to pee in a cup.

As a man,
I'll never get used to…

Having my freedom,
Taken away.

Brother

Brother where you been
All my life?

The streets got you
Dancing with
Trouble and strife,

The gun and the knife
And I ain't been living so
Right myself.

I think this generation's
Cursed, I think we need
Some help.

A little rehabilitation,
Hospitals and
Police Stations filled
With our young nation,

It's us that made them,
It's mayhem.

Destined to the pen,
So I use my pen,
Try and start again,

Tell you
What's happening
And what's good.

It's all hood,
In the hood.

All wearing hoods,
Trying to be the next
Clint Eastwood,
Guns are blazing.

Leave you bleeding,
On the pavement,
No remorse, of course,
Another corpse,

The minds warped,
Too much TV,
Too much drugs.

I think my telephone's
Bugged, I'm paranoid.

When it's me and my boys,
We talk in code.

Code of the road,
Plans unfold.

On how we can make it,
Street or the music,

Don't wanna confuse it,

Na...but it's like,
They're one and the same,

Remember my name,
Syrus ain't gon'
Come here again.

1st strike and changing
My lane,
Quick all the same.

And it's a shame,

You're living in a
Concrete cell

And it's a shame
You're on road
And still living in hell.

And it's a shame,
No one wants to
Change their ways.

And it's a shame,
Cause it's the
End of days,

The trumpet blows,
I done seen the light,
The strength the might,
The shield the sword.

I ask the Lord
To guide my lyrics,
I want my
Brother to hear it.

Know your older's
Praying for you,

We conversate
on a visit.

Right now
We're going through the
Same thing,
Just on different wings.

You go hold down 'D'
And I'm a hold down 'B,'
Like you used to
Hold down Brixton
And I used to
Hold down Heath.

In Ere

Man dem don't get
No Birthdays in ere!

Man dem don't get
No Christmas in ere!

Man dem don't get
No New Years

In ere, in ere, in ere,
In ere, in ere!

Drama's a daily occurrence,

Man threaten man,
To send man
To their parents.

Like they know addresses
And postal codes.

That beef 's personal,
That beef 's from road.

Or that's some kitty argument
Don't bring it to me.

HMP will be
The last place you see,
Believe me.

In ere,
Calls are like a pound a minute,

So you sneak a techno
On a ...visit,

Or pay a price that's ridiculous,

But it's worth
The phone sex
With your Mrs.

When you're handling
Your biz, you better
Watch for them snitches.

In ere,
Some walk around
Like they're shook,

Maybe they're scared of
The hot oil,

Scared of the jook.

In ere,
Wifey's picture stays by my head,

In ere
I pray to the lord,
Don't let my people dead.

In ere,
I think about
All my mistakes,

In ere, in ere, in ere
In ere, in ere!

Game Of Life

Sometimes I just sit,
Watching time go by.

Sitting in a corner
Light beaming on my A4.

I play chess with my peers,
Real life war.

Pawn or a King,
Foreseeing your next move.

I bowl for the strike,
Why you rolling in the groove?

Positivity
Puts me in the right mood.

I wanna get back
To the hot spot,

Where it's all warm,
Place I call home.

I'm a code my shit,
Listen for the drop.

I'm a listen to my critics,
Tell me what's what.

But I can't be judged,
I've got to overstand.

Got to teach my teachers
We can cure the land.

Why do our profits,
Seem to get dammed?

When the glass breaks,
What will happen to the sand?

Stronger force,
Paper, stone, scissor
With the hand?

Wind, water, fire,
Lyrics fuel my desire.

Snakes take you under,

While the ladder
Takes you higher!

Climb up my people,
I'm a meet you at the top,

Full circle of knowledge,
Make this bullshit stop.

Rastaman's Cell

I got Muslims to the left of me,
Atheists to the right.

I'm in the Rastaman's cell,
I'm gonna pray tonight.

I got the Psalms and the Quaran,
Filling my head.

I'm trying to overstand Selassie I,
Ras not Dread.

Okay,
Read a little more.

I don't need a Muslim Rug,
To put my knees down on the floor.

I don't need a history book
To know why... certain people poor.

And if I turn the other cheek,
They'll call me 2 faced for sure.

And I used to want a gang,
But I don't want that no more.

I got my friends and family,
I guess I've matured.

Gangs don't protect,
Gangs only create war.

Survival of the fittest,
I just ran for an hour.

Shoulders have to broad
And mid section narrow.

Counting my packs,
Like I need 2 more.

Increasing the reps
On the bed and on the floor.

My motivation...
Protect the neck and crack the jaw.

Confined

I was confined within brick walls
And an old style barred window.

A large, blue metal door
That hardly ever opened.
The cream paint, traced and softened
The hard brick.

We decorated our peripherals,
With visions that appealed.

Topless models in the early days.

Ordered to take them down,
New regulations again.

Blue pin striped shirts
And dirty mops.

Cake and custard,
In a plastic bowl,

To be ate with a plastic spoon.

Tomorrow will be the same as
Yesterday.

Books and imagination is everything.

Reality TV…

Fascinating!

Move On

Today nothing happened,
Nothing moved, nothing stirred.

I slept through the hours,
And spoke very few words.

Checked the date,
Checked the time,
Checked the TV guide.

TV and music
Will help me through this HMP ride.

When your life is no longer your own,
Everything can seem surreal.

Like a car crashing into you,
Sending you flying in the air.

To wake up on a hospital bed,
Wondering how you got there.

Behind this closed door,
I ask myself the same question.

And put it down to
Association, informers and investigation.

No time to cry,
Life goes on.

Learn from mistakes
And swiftly move on.

Free Internally

I spit better than you,
I'm waiting on you,

To tighten your aim.

All that money
And fame.

Ain't a thing,
If you're broke,
On the inside.

A joke,
On the inside.

Ain't got a clue,
What it's like
On the inside.

I live from the inside,
Speak from the inside.

Before I die on the out,
I'd die from the inside.

That's my spirit
And my soul now.

Lost it a bit,
But back in control now.

Who doesn't fall foul,
To the trappings
Of this world.

She's like every girl,
I don't trust her,

She's trying
To deceive me.

Everything that
Glitters ain't gold,

So I'm watching
Her closely.

Swear I won't slip again,
Swear I won't
Cheat again.

What goes around,
Comes right back
Around again.

So I'm on
A straight ting,
Done all the bait ting.

The worlds a bitch,
So you better watch
The rape ting.

If we're talking road,
Then you better watch
The Jake ting.

That's the
Police boy dem and
The snake ting.

Quick to set you up
And chat behind
Your back ting.

Yeah this
Brother's hurting,

But he don't know
How to cry

And he don't know
How to lie.

So he spits lyrics,
With a venom
From the inside.

I don't think you
Hear my cries,
I don't think
You're listening.

I'm like the breeze
Through the trees,
Just whistling.

Ooh that's
A pretty sound,
That's a nice melody.

But Hurricane Mitch
Was, oh so deadly,

The cancer, the H.I.V,
The infant mortality.

Can't be free on the out,
Till you're free internally.

Father

We needed to spend
Time together,

Reason with one another.

Learn from the ways
Of my father,

That's my laughter,
That's my pain.

Share our doubts,
As well as our last name.

Wouldn't change a thing,
Don't get me wrong.

The man of the house,
Is supposed to be strong.

Chose to be an artist,
Paint picture through song.

Knowing that words,
Can't test the action.

Mother Africa

Mother like Africa,
The centre of my earth
You gave me birth.

Eagerly awaited my first words.

Took me from the nurse,
How did it come to this?

The system's got me now,
I reminisce.

On days when I was
A little younger,
I never starved,

But still had that hunger,

To be amongst the
Highly paid.

Even if it took me to my grave,
I wouldn't change my ways,

Slowly watched my youth fade away.

Incarcerated up until today,
It won't be forever.

Every time I call,
She'd feel better.

Sharing fate with my brother,

Tell my sister I love her,
How she must wonder.

How her brothers are so,
Grimed out and crimed out.

Forced to take a little time out.

But everything for a reason,
16 more seasons,

Balance some good with the bad
And make it even.

Keep Loving Your Son

Mother keep loving your son,
I'm doing well.

You always knew I would make it,
I could tell.

You look me in my eyes,
Asked me what I'm doing now,

You heard about the most foul,
But I'm still your child.

Been through it,

I wanna enjoy my journey.

Communicate my mind,
Through voice delivery.

The enraged caged lion,
Still resides in me…

Seems I got
Nowhere to go.

Isis

Nia my daughter,
Black diamond
You shine.

Isis my sister,
Strong heart
And strong mind.

Africa my mother,
Centre of all
Where life began.

You were neglected
By your King,
Disrespected and forgotten.

You were neglected by your King,
Laid aside, like ripe fruit,
Left to rotten.

You were not carried to and fro,
Catered to hand and toe.

You were not serenaded daily,
Protected from this harsh world.

So to you so much is due.

I apologise to you my Queen,
For all your heartache
And your pain.

I apologise to you my Queen,
For not calling you by your name.

I apologise to you my Queen,
Although blind I still can see.

That your strength is
Immeasurable,

That your resilience is
Unmatched.

That your beauty is heaven sent

And that for me you are
Perfectly matched.

Aura's Gleam

I used to hear planes
And think the world
Was coming to an end.

I used to sleep
Thinking I would
Never wake again.

And now I blink
The window of
My opportunity.

Look a little deeper,
Explore my history.

The pyramids show
The secrets above,

13 doesn't mean death,
It means love,

They're cloning us!

Test it on the animals.
But I'm an animal,
A mammal,
A being.

A human being,
Or being seen...uh.

They're watching us,
Watching you,
Watching me.

Entertain us
With our own end,
It's TV.
"What?"

My food get seasoned,
Likes there's four.

My people reason,
Cause there's more.

They don't like it,
So there's war.

Eating apples
To the core,
I'm eating apples
To the core.

Hey yo,
I walk with
A few good men,
A chosen few.

It's beef you want
With them?

It's beef I want
With you.

Trying to stop my flow,
A fork in the road,

I hear your Morse code.

Story gets deeper,
Story untold.

Advancement
Slowly unfolds.

What was written
Was read,

Make up your
Own mind.

Then place your cards
On the table,
Play with my kind.

We creators,
Rule breakers,
Move makers and such.

We breaking
Through shackles and
Ripping off handcuffs.

Shit ain't always
What it seems,
But we definitely
Following dreams.

Step back and watch
My aura gleam...

Step back and watch
My aura gleam.

Cry For The Dead

I don't cry for the dead.

I cry cause I know,
I'm gonna miss them instead.

Cause my boy's just gone,
Na, my boy just went.

Went to see the maker.

My boy's life spent,
Chasing the paper.

But what does it matter now,
He's chilling with the Creator.

Listen, I got unbreakable faith,

There's no one that can tell me
That my God's not great

And there's not a better place,
After here.

I see their faces
In my mind,

Then they disappear.

I picture…
A beach, with a perfect blue sky.

People hugging one another,
So why should I cry?

Feel sorry for them,
I feel sorry for myself.

But I still miss you,
Went on my knees and knelt.

Asked the Lord,
To watch over your spirit

And you left some children here,
So for them I really feel it.

But don't watch nothing,
You've got my word.

I'm a watch over them,
When I get back to the curb.

Live For The Living

Live for the living.
Live while the living's good.

I'm a,
Live for the living.
Live while the living's good.

I'm living for my
Mother and father.

I'm living for my unborn son
And my unborn daughter.

I'm living for my
Brother and sisters,
Uncles and aunties,
Cousins that swarm me,

This is my family.

I'm living for my
Friends that passed.

I'm living for the
Children in Africa,

That don't have a chance.

I'm living for all those
With hope.

I'm living for those,

Hooked on the brown
And hooked on the coke.

I'm living for those
Locked up all day.

23hrs a day,
Till their skin turns pale.

That's why I'm alive
And don't give up at night.

I accept the dark,
So I can receive the light.

I'm living for those,
That know the truth.

I got the answers in me,
You got the answers in you!

(A)llow Them Endz

Ever felt like (a)llow them endz,
Them endz ain't mine.

Ever felt like (a)llow them friends,
Them friends ain't mine.

Ever been betrayed,
Wishing you could press rewind.

Return to yesterday,
When everything was fine.

Well never mind,
Love hurts

And life is hard.

But you wouldn't
Wanna miss it,

Better play your cards.

Take charge.
Sometimes we lead,
Sometimes we follow.

When death comes a knocking,
They say nobody knows.

Real Big Man

This ain't no little man spit,
This is big man tings.

Talking cars, ice, homes
That man parades in.

I'm in a league of my own,
My world is flossy.

I got murderers
In my pocket,
So I dare you to push me.

I'm untouchable, bullet proof,
A girl's wet dream.

I'm a shotter by trade,
Quickly serve up the fiends.

But you know the saying,
Every dog has his day.

When gravity kicks in,
All debts have to be paid.

Cause you reaped so long
And you never did sow.

Checking your reflection
And you just don't know.

What you thought was important,
Ain't important no more.

When you reason with the rich
And realise that they're poor.

The re-occurring question,
What the F is it for?

Like,
Why we do this,

And why we do that.

One size fits all.

But there's
More than one cap.

The Letter

I was a victim of the game,
Not a player of the game.

What I saw hardened me.

Before the door closed,
Before the hammer rose,
Before the last kiss.

I was already numb inside.

So by the time,
Destination met fate.

I didn't care enough to weep.

I deserved and desired it.

Held my chin up high,
Ready to ride it.

It took about 3 years.
A letter from Charmaine.

Before I released my guard.

I thought about her life,
I thought of my niece.

I felt my guilt.

I embraced the welling,
As I breathed

And allowed the tears to fall.

It was a symbol…

That I was alive,
That I cared

And that my feelings were real.

2 Pac & Nas

I find it soothing
To here man
Speak to God.

That's why I listen
To 2 Pac and Nas,

While driving fast cars
Or laying in
My cell at night.

I listen carefully,
I hear their plight,
I hear their strife,
I hear their life.

I love music,
Our communication,

My salvation,

It's not just me.
That battles,
This good and
Bad in me.

A killer with dreams,
A shotter with fiends,
Jack with them beans.

There's no
Beanstalks here,
Just murder and war.

You wanna join
The army,
What for?

There's gangs outside.

Not eager to recruit.
But eager to shoot,

Don't be a target.
Wanna leave it,

But I feel like
I'm a part of it.

Like that's my scene,
And that's my home.

Like,
There's the food,
And there's the chrome.

Protect it with your life
And own the throne.

But there's no castle.

Just a judge and jury,
To laugh at you.

And give you your
Time to serve.

Mothers cry,
But can't find the word.

Sons raised on the curb

We got our own
Rules out here.

We don't practise
What we preach,
Like a Bush or a Blair.

So hypocritical,

Or maybe cause we left
What was,
Oh so natural.

Each one teach one,
But I'm a bad example.

Each one teach one,
I could've done better.

The Edge

We sharing weather people,
Under the sun.

We giants of the earth,
Since the dinosaurs gone.

Opposites attract,
I recognise sun through rain.

Only for a season,
Then it comes round again.

I rejoice in my chance,
To put things right.

Made clumsy mistakes,
Walked the blade of life.

"Don't slip" mamma called,
"Don't slip" father yelled.

Don't worry,
God will catch me,
Before I end up in hell.

Night Time Vision

I bring you knowledge
From my subliminal
Night time vision.

Take heed, indecision
Leaves you cripple.

I ripple through the world,

Like baby's step in water.
Necessary evil,
Cows to slaughter?

Adopted you
Brought daughter.

Figures no father.
Eastender's drama,
Reality saga.

I'm gonna hit you
That much harder.
You ready?
Grab your honour.

Shielded ready for battle.

Babies rattle, rattling,
Rush adrenaline,
Symbolism re-appearing,

Stop staring.

The glare is ridiculous.

Domino effect,
This could be infectious.

Well then follow me,
On this reciprocal ride,

All aboard
Churrp, churrp
Ride or die.

Ruff riding iga,
Driving iga.

Uncomfortable
In passenger side,

Not in full control of my
Own f-ing ride.
So watch me roll,

Cruise control,
With no button.

Close my eyes, I'm not
Killing nut'em,
I'm saying sut'em.

I've been guided.
Faith manifesting
My future,

Survival on the tip
Of my tongue,
A man now.

Maturity stemming
From my lungs,

Where's my
Innocence gone?
This is no longer fun.

Consequence,
I've got to eat it,

Food Sunday to Sunday
Daily struggle
Starting From Monday,

Free maybe one day.
Last days
When I can truly live.

Received life,
Woman's gift to give.
Woman's gift to give?

Or a punishment,
Who really decides?

Judgement day,
I can't wait.
I love competition.

Sinners it be you,
I'd be joining or missing.

Hold on,
You need dusting,
You're white with fear.

I got people I can't wait
Make disappear.

Wars un-squashed,
But did they ever
Really start.

Beef between
The mind and the heart.
The mind and the heart.

Ocean Blue

I wanna run
To the end of my path
And choose sides.

Embed myself
In the ocean blue
And stay alive.

The calm,
The simplicity.

The danger,
The mystery.

Spread my wings
To the surface,

At last I'm free.

I'm the eagle,
The dolphin,
The Midas Touch.

When you're
Head over heels,
You say
I love you so much.

What's love?

Love is meaning
Without word.

What's love?

Love is needing
So much it hurts.

What's love?

Love is giving your best.

Withstanding
Life's pressures
And passing times test.

And I've never been
In love before,

How could I?
I never did wanna
Give more,

Why should I?
Maybe there's time
For me yet.

Loneliness will be the
Only regret,
I don't fret.

Cause the gift
Of the gab's,
Gonna get me through.

And when I see
You on the road,
Can I talk to you?

The Oath

Till dust in eternity,
I solemnly swear.

To stick to the rules
That got me here.

Like honour thy code
And return back.

The love given to me,
Cause I love that.

We unify through the tears,
That we shared in the past.

Your picture etched in my mind,
So it's built to last.

Your deeds recorded in my memory,
Remember me!

I held ground with ya,
We made history.

And although the future's cloudy,
I'm a tell you straight.

I don't regret none of my life,
I learnt through every mistake.

I'm a teach who'll listen,
I'm a leader at heart.

I watch my path carefully,
I spit light in the dark.

Now that you see
What I'm talking about,

I'm the loudest quiet soldier
That you knew from South.

And I done travelled
Round the world,
So don't cry for me.

Seen bloody elbows and knees,
Real poverty.

So while we're
Starving under chandeliers
And leather seats.

I'm a stop and meditate
And try to find some peace.

A Moment's Worth

One life to live,
Don't give it away.

Look around
Cause today's the day,

The moment's now.
Make a vow,

To honour and cherish
The minutes.

The hour wouldn't stand a chance,
If the seconds didn't tick.

So it's worthy,
Like stretching before a fight.

Yeah it's worthy,
Like praying before the night.

Oh yeah, it's worthy,
Like thank you and sorry dear.

If it wasn't worthwhile,
Then I wouldn't be here.

Have A Look

Brave new world,
The keepers of the watch.

Everything around,
That you see,

Was ordained.
For poetry.

The orange peel
Against the wood.

The coco butter cream,
For your skin.

The clear see through bag,
Enveloping the bin.

I see green sheets
And fairy liquid,

I see hope…

And the future
In our kids.

Acknowledgements

First and foremost I thank the Most High
for my wonderful blessings and ask
to be continually guided into finding my purpose.

To my beautiful wife Rosalind,
thank you for my precious son and for being the love of my life.

To my friends and
family who have stood by me and encouraged me throughout,
you know who you are, nuff love always.

Thanks to all who gave me valuable feedback and advice in particular
Janelle for your great energy, ideas and creativity.

Thanks to the Blantyre House Education and Resettlement Team
who supported what I wanted to achieve, in particular
Debbie Leach, Penny Lowe and Steve Harris.

To the organisations that I came into contact with, your work has
great value and purpose in providing second chances.
To the Prisoners Education Trust, St Giles Trust,
Foundation4Life and GOALS UK, I am
forever grateful.

To those that haven't come home, stay focused and positive, freedom is
a must, special mention Fatla, Spencer, Joe, Mo, Biggs & Osei.

we are all capable of achieving great things.
The first step is to believe that
you can.

Love, peace and blessings!

Glossary

Africa	Egyptian word for Motherlan...
Aggro	Slang term for aggressiv...
Akhoy(a)s	Pronounced Ackee is the Arabic term for brothe... The Muslim culture in jail has great unity and strengt...
(A) llow	The A has been bracketed to keep it silent for sound emphasi...
Bait	To do something that will undoubtedly lead to you getting into troubl...
Beef	To fight or to wa...
Biz	Short hand for business, legal or otherwis...
Brown	Heroine, a choice drug in prison due to the docile effe... and the relatively shorter time the drug is detectabl... when providing urine sample...
Bun out	A Rastafarian saying to cleanse by fir...
Bus case	To be found not guilty after trial or on appea...
Chrome	Meaning gu...
Curb	The road, indicating freedo...
Donkey	Someone who does something risky for others, for a pa... off or through intimidatio...
Ere	Shortening of word 'Here,' the H has bee... left off for sound emphasi...
Flossy	To be able to afford expensive material item...
Fiend	Someone addicted to drug...
Food	Meaning drug...
Gang	In this sense is a group formed to commit crime. There ar... many groups formed for positive outcome...
Grimed Out	To not care, to be outcas...
Hood	Place of povert...

Glossary

Iga	Shortening of the derogatory N word,which groups like N.W.A and artists like 2 Pac and Nas reclaimed.
Insha'Allah	Arabic for God willing, the beauty of the language influences. many non Muslims to communicate in this holy way.
Isis	Woman of the throne.
Jake's	Slang term for police or rhyming slang for snakes.
Jook	To be stabbed with sharp object.
Kitty	Someone addicted to drugs.
Move To	To approach with violent intentions.
Nia	Means radience and brightness.
Overstand	Means you fully get the discussion and the deeper Meaning and remain a powerful individual.
Paper	Slang term for money.
Pen	Means prison, from the American term Penitentiary.
Rastarfari	Ras means Head, Tafari means he who inspires.
Reason	To have deep and meaningful conversation.
Shook	Someone who is scared or shows fear.
Shotter	Someone who sells drugs.
Snake	Someone who can not be trusted.
Social & Domestic	Is the 45min to an hour that you have to make phone. calls and have a shower. You can socialise in this time.
Yardie	Slang term for someone from Jamaica, some may find the term derogarory, this was not the intention.

A Note On The Author

Christopher Syrus is the Director of Syrus Consultancy C.I.C, an initiative created to influence young people through personal development, mentoring and creative art workshops.

LoveLife6958 is the symbolic transformation of his allocated prison number LL6958, representing the change from his negative past towards a promising and positive future.

Christopher has dedicate himself to working with young people enabling them to learn from his mistakes. During his sentence he studied Psychology with the Open University, completed an NVQ in Advice and Guidance, 7303 Teacher Training and Goals for Young People facilitation. For his accomplishments he was awarded the 2008 Learning Skills Council 'Achieving Against The Odds' award.

Christopher has received many accolades for his work in the community. He has been given the honored role of patron for 'Mothers Against Guns', awarded the 'Turn Around' Peace Award 2010 and in 2012 awarded 'Croydon's Next Top Role Model,' from 'C.A.C.F.O' (Croydon African Caribbean Family Organisation). As a spoken word artist his 'LoveLife6958 Acoustic Band' delivers crime prevention tours, to schools and youth establishments nationally, his short film 'LoveLife6958 Memoirs from the pen...' achieved Platinum Award from leading prison charity 'Koestler Trust.'

The book and workshops are testimony to his self belief and determination to give back to the community, inspire young people and to have personal success in a field that he is passionate about, believing that with the right guidance young people that are vulnerable and/or disaffected can become law abiding, successful members of the community, achieving their personal goals.

For more info: www.syrusconsultancy.com

Notes

LoveLife6958 Memoirs from the pen... is collection of poems written while serving a prison sentence. They detail the journey from Kingston Crown Court, through to the 23 hour lock down in HMP Wandsworth and other UK prisons. The title LoveLife6958 is the symbolic transformation of the prison number LL6958. In sharing the experience this book serves as a deterrent from crime and also speaks of the hope and power of change.

Christopher Syrus is an author, spoken word artist and motivational speaker. As the founder of Syrus Consultancy C.I.C - Delivering Creative Youth Services, Christopher is committed to the empowerment and personal development of young people through the creative arts.

Chris Syrus

'It has a stop - start effect on the emotion. One time you are in the middle of something painful, the next time love, the next time spiritual... Some of the most beautiful and profound lines anyone could ever wish to write'
Chickenshed

'Inspiring and a deterrent as it shows the wrong path is not worth it.'
LIVE Magazine

Delivering Creative Youth Services

www.syrusconsultancy.com

ISBN: 978-1-907188-80-0

9 781907 188800

£8.99